# SPIRITUAL

# AWAK👀NING

# SPIRITUAL
# AWAK👀NING

Kimberlyn D. Leader

Library of Congress Control Number :     2018901035
ISBN:          Hardcover                 978-1-5434-8082-5
               Softcover                 978-1-5434-8081-8
               eBook                     978-1-5434-8080-1

Print information available on the last page.

Rev. date: 02/15/2018

**To order additional copies of this book, contact:**
Xlibris
1-888-795-4274
www.Xlibris.com
Orders@Xlibris.com
773896

# CONTENTS

# INTRODUCTION

I give thanks to so many people that inspired me. Those that caused a great impact In my life, believed and supported me. To the love of my life and my foundation, my parents Gerald and Bessie Mae Leader. I've been blessed to had both parents in the household along with 5 sisters 3 brothers nieces nephews along with a host of outside children that my parents raised that made us a large Leader family. They last name didn't have to be Leader, if you was raised in my household you are automatically a Leader. To be a Leader is to love respect and support that we gave to one another. Thankful that my parents kept a solid strict but loving home, disciplined but well rooted and grounded. The values, love and respect that they embedded in my life carried me through and made me the strong spiritual woman that I am today. My circle is limited but the loving souls that God made apart of my life that helped me along the way; guided, feed, supported and embraced me. To my three beautiful Children that I love so dearly. Shanice Tenika McClure, John Patrick McClure Jr and Jaquan Gerald McClure who are my blessing and my completion. They installed in my heart and showed me how to love unconditionally and also to become a strong successful independent black woman. Forever the three love of my life that keeps my heart beating.

My first love and through infinity my Heavenly Father, my Lord and Savior Jesus Christ and the Holy Spirit that I am made one with. Forever thankful, stand humble and walk with my Lord as a child of God through the Holy Spirit. Life has been a challenge with many turbulences and unfamiliar spirits that invaded my life; trying to make its way to destroy me so many times. But God released his mighty power, his grace and mercy that brought me through and to live life fearful in him but wonderfully made through my heavenly Father. I can do all things through Christ which strengthened me and writing this book is the beginning to what has just begun in my life and the many blessings to come. In the name of Jesus.

# Chapter 1

# IN THE BEGINNING

Let's take it back to the beginning. See we all have a beginning and a ending; the question is who and what you become during this process and to know that we are giving one of God's greatest gift. LIFE

Father God I ask of you to help those who are blind allow them to see, those who are rebellious allow them to be receptive to your holy spirit. Hearts that's are harden give their life to you. You are our Alpha and Omega our beginning and our end. I pray that this book can make a difference. As I hold this book up towards the heavens asking of you Heavenly Father through this book speak to your children and allow them to hear your voice. Help those to not only be hearers but doers of your word. Deliver those out of darkness and into the grace and mercy of your hands. Through your light bring life into the lives of those unsaved souls. We cannot do anything without you and through you all things are possible. As many that knows the truth, hear and obey your word, set theirs souls free. Allow them to live and not to live just to die.

Like so many I have questioned and asked "Who am I and what is my life purpose here on earth". Was I born just to wait and die. What happens in between. Why is life so hard. So many took these questions and other questions and live life based on trying to figure it out. Those that never did took it to their grave. So many people wakes up physically alive but spiritual dead. Confused, angry depressed, hateful and destructive which are negative spiritual energy that takes over many lives and has them walking dead. So who are we, what is our purpose, what's keeping us alive physically mentally and spiritually. Why are there so many that's in command or of Authority use their powers to strip the less fortunate, uses their authority to destroy and/or take away lives. Why is there so many people that gets in the minds of the weak, brainwash them to hate one another, steal from those who work so hard to get what little they have. Along with jealousy, envy, back biting, strife and hate. As long as those who continues to do it in their own selfish ways they will continue to struggle to find satisfaction and peace. The more money that they get the more money that they want. Many that walks around that react to these feelings; I'm not satisfied with one or two cars I need multiple of cars. One woman or one man cannot do much for me I need that side relationship to give me what my spouse or significant other is not giving me. I need me a drink time and time and a hit once in awhile. As long as I keep it hidden stay quite about it no one will know. We all have been their one way or another and many of us are still there. This is why the world has a saying "We all have those skeletons in our closets". The flesh is never satisfied. The more you feed it the more it wants. The flesh that stands weak stands alone. Many actually has a tendency of believing that they can live life in this world alone and don't need anybody else. Where as many that holds so much pride confessing in their heart, I've worked hard for this, I build this Empire by myself, when there wasn't anybody there for me I made it through by myself. Others that will confess; if it wasn't for me you wouldn't be where you are now. Due to this pride many are walking around building this throne that makes them believe that they are the creator of this world. See you don't have to say it but you are living a lifestyle that says it for you. I can walk around with a guns;

I can't be touched. If anything they will go down before I will. If I have my kids from different baby daddies that's cool because I can make my money by getting child support from all of them. I have all these babies mommas out there, I give them a few dollars to help them take care of those kids, make a few booty calls to shut them up and still do me. How many times we have heard it. Many are still walking with that lifestyle today. Due to the ways of the world and how it's set up, more so then ever, for corruption and failure. Corruptive politics, non justice for the right of the righteous, the hunger and greed of money, sexual lusting for one another, all this to say these corrupted ways lead to ones failure and eventually being SPIRITUALLY DEAD. We have rights but not always being performed. Voices but it's not being heard and many that are Intelligent but yet not being recognized. Our children that's being labelled, drugged up and unfortunately dying in the hands of the very one's that should be protecting them. Again all this is to say so many are just living waiting to die. They don't know which way to turn and where they stand. So they question "What is my purpose here on earth". Do I give up before I even try. Even to the one's that believed to be fortunate with the riches of their money, college degrees, fine homes and cars, talented, gifted, multiple relationship with women and/or men or both but yet unfortunately they hold such high rate of suicide. What is it to have everything you want and still not happy. Continue seeking searching needing wanting that's what mankind is doing. Looking for an answer and trying to find a way out. Again why is it that so many are not happy. Why is it when we think we got it all together and everything is going our way and then with a blink of an eye many have lose everything or back to square one. Causing many to turned to drugs and alcohol for the answer or to cover up their pain. Using these substances to not deal with life situations or help them to forget the pain but yet the soul continues to cry out. When does it stop or does it stop. Will it get worst before it gets better. These are questions that we should be asking ourselves and what can we do to help make life better.

PEOPLE HEAR ME; MONEY DRUGS/ALCOHOL SEX FAMILY/FRIENDS POLITICS SPORTS etc…these things or people are not the answer. Wake up and stop trying to do it your way. Some folks really think that they got it all figured out. Worshipping money and power as their god. Taking their position in leadership to control and brainwash people to serve and follow them. There are even though that knows God, takes his words uses it to dehumanize people. Overall God states, through the lack of knowledge we perish. This is why it is so important to have a relationship with God and to know his word. To obtain wisdom and knowledge of his word through his Holy Spirit and in him, only him, should we serve.

## HOSEA 4:6

(6) My people are destroyed from lack of knowledge. Because you have rejected knowledge, I also reject you as my priest; because you have ignored the law of God, I will ignore your children.

When one chooses to live in the natural, living in darkness, walking around lost and confused, seeking their own pleasure and the ways of the world; as a result one will live but yet walk spiritually like the walking dead. Know that we are fighting a Spiritual Warfare. Our fight is not each other nor is it money power or even the President of the United States. As in the beginning of human kind, our fight is between Good and Evil.

## EPHESIANS 6:11-13

(11) Put on the whole armour of God, that ye may be able to stand against the wiles of the devil.

(12) For we wrestle not against flesh and blood, but against principalities, powers, against the rulers of the darkness of this world, against spiritual wickedness in high places.

(13) Wherefore take unto you the whole armour of God, that ye may be able to withstand in the evil days, that and having done all, to stand.

We must give our life to God, walk in the spirit. With the Spirit of God then will you hear God, your purpose/God's purpose for you. Without God in your life there's no since of direction. It will be a losing battle because we cannot fight this spirit that devour the earth on our own. I was lead by the spirit of God to write this book and without my Lord and Savior it would have been impossible. Accepting Jesus Christ as my Lord and Savior I no longer have to fight this battle on my own, he fights for me. I am a conquer, overcome from the darkness of this world, spiritually healed and now I live. I had to shut down the natural ways of the world and surround myself with and in the Spirit of God. Walking with the Holy Spirit led me not into my own understanding but in the perfect will of God.

6

## PROVERBS 3:5-6

(5) Trust in the Lord with all thine heart: and lean not unto thine own understanding. In all thy ways acknowledge him and he shall direct thy paths.

(6) I am made one with the Holy Spirit of God and in him do I trust.

Understand the body is just a shield that comes in different colors shapes and sizes. It starts out new gets old and die. Unfortunately so many never made it to that older stage. But the spirit is everlasting along with that God gives us a free will and our own state of mind. Giving us our own choices and with that atheist is on the rise. Unbelievers (lack of knowledge and understanding) made their choices to not believe in God. Then you have those without a chance sold their soul over to the devil. Let's go back and touch base to the beginning from the foundation because that where knowledge begins.

## GENESIS 1:1

In the Beginning God created the Heaven and the Earth

## GENESIS 1:26 & 27

(26) And God said, let us make man in OUR image, after OUR likeness.

(27) So God created man in his own image, in the image of God created he in him; male and female created he them.

We know that God is a spirit. He created us in his image and in the spiritual formed that dwells in the body. See the body will die but the spirit is everlasting. Money, Title, Degrees, Food, Material Things etc... These worldly things are giving to us through the Grace of God to enjoy and allow us to be happy through our visit here on earth. Not these things to become our god. When we die we are not going to take these things with us and we will stand on Judgement day to face our everlasting God thy Father. The Devil is not our creator but has a job to do: steal, kill and destroy. As much as we hate the devil's work he's out to do his job as where the son of God (our Lord and Savior) came down and did his job. He was Baptist with the Holy Spirit, shed his blood so we are healed, crucified to save mankind and now sit at the right hand of the Father. We to are created to do a job so becoming one with the Lord we to should know as an individual what is our job and purpose here on earth.

When God stated in Genesis 1:26 LET US MAKE MAN IN OUR IMAGE. "US" Who you think God was talking to? His son Jesus Christ who sat with him from the beginning of time making all things possible and through him all things that was made was made by him. But mankind turns around and give the devil to much credit along with family, friends, Leadership of all kinds, statues, hell even the Universe with its big bang Theory. Many have chosen to love these things, people and all other kinds of walk of life so much that they made it as serving it as their god(s). We are killing each other, killing ourselves, destroying the Land, corrupting and poisoning our water and food, polluting the air etc...etc...and what one do is blaming it all on the devil. Again God give us our own mind and free will. It's just the question on what and who you choose to serve and how you choose to use your mind. I believe that one of the most serious problem that one faces is trying to serve two Masters at the same time; leaving those speaking double talking and a confuse mind. Trust and believe that life is really not that hard. People choose to make it hard because of their walk in life. When you walk with God in your life, trust and believe, in him you will find that the life that God gives you in the body is to live heaven right here on earth. Until the day of your calling to your permanent home where life in the spirit becomes the place of peace and everlasting life.

# Chapter 2

# WE CANNOT SERVE TWO MASTERS

## MATTHEW 6:24

(24) No man can serve two Masters: For either he will hate the one, and love the other; or else he will hold to the one, and despise the other. Ye cannot serve God and Mammon. I would like to touch base on this particular topic because so many people are living this double life, basically trying to serve two Masters. We got many in Leadership, of Authority, in The Poll Pit, even men and women that has been called by God to serve him and to perform his works. Many has taking their calling, their gift and handed it over to the devil. Walking along with his demons and turning that same power that God grant them, to confuse and/or destroy other people. They use God's word to capture minds, take away and/or turn God words around to satisfy their own lust. Even down to their own God gifted talent to poison souls and getting those to turn their soul over to the devil. Now we have those that are called "Lukewarm Souls". These people are selective in the word of God. They select God's word making themselves to appear to be Holy. They may go to Church, quote God's word, called themselves filled with the Holy Spirit and/or appear to have people believing that they are living Holy and righteously. But these are the same ones that you will find at night clubs, bars, in the bed with different men, women, children and even animals. Drinking drugging and the list goes on and on...God allows me to speak this because again; WE CANNOT SERVE TWO MASTERS. I

chuckle because this brings me back to a comedian back in the days by the name of Flip Wilson. When he use to act out a scene that was ungodly. The first thing he would say is "The Devil made me do it" How many continue to live this hypocritical double life and when they get caught blames it on the Devil. Pretty much saying, "The devil made me do it". Again let me emphasize, The devil is doing his job; to steal kill and destroy". The devil has that power over you only if you give him the power. You control your life. You have to take responsibility on what you do, how you walk as a person and the decisions you make, makes you who you are. Keep in mind for whatever you feed your spirit that's what going to come out in your actions and speaks out from the soul. Substance might vacate from the body in a different format from how it was put in, but after it's been broken down that same substance will eventually exit the body. Well the same thing applies to what you feed the spirit. For whatever you feed the spirit, after it's has been processed and broken down it will exit from the mouth leaving one to confess and walk in that path. Negative or positive whatever spiritual energy one chooses to live by so one will stand.

PROVERBS 23:7

(7) For as he thinketh in his heart, so is he:

If you accepting NEGATIVE words and NEGATIVE energy NEGATIVITY you will live. If you build a life circle around selfish, angry, hatred NEGATIVE people NEGATIVE you shall become.

If you accepting POSITIVE energy, and surrounding yourself with positive, caring and loving people you will likely have a POSITIVE attitude with a POSITIVE Lifestyle.

Like minds and spirits do connect and by choice if you walk in the spirit of God you shall connect with him being as one with The Father The Son and The Holy Spirit. Then shall you live. By choice if you dancing with the devil and his demons surely you will die. ARE YOU LIVING JUST WAITING TO DIE.

Again let me touch base back to the beginning because this is where knowledge and understanding begins. We were all born in sin and fall short of the glory of God. As a young Christian this message dwelled in my spirit. We was born into this sinful world and this is why it is so important that we give our children back to the Heavenly Father in spirit and to pray for our children souls. At one point in my life having my children I've experience something with my first born child, that I end up later calling it "The B.T.T" which means Baby Temptation Tantrum. I had my first born and only daughter Shanice Tenika Bessie McClure. She had to be about one year old during this time. Now before I begin this story we know that when a child is born the first taste that the child will get will be the taste of milk. Either it's going to be breast milk or formula milk, this is what's going to nurture and bring satisfaction to the child. So now at 1 year old Shanice is well familiar with milk and like all babies will cry when she feels hungry. So she was sitting in his high chair waiting to be feed. I walked over to her with her sippy cup with milk in one hand and I had a bottle of Pink Champagne in the other hand for myself. Now of course she's familiar with the cup of Milk but she saw this unfamiliar bottle in my hand. So she started reaching out for it. So when I told her no and the stubborn child that she was, she started crying kicking and throwing a tantrum. I try giving her the cup of milk but she threw it on the floor and proceed to cry out louder. Making attempts to give her the milk again and again she continue to throw it on the floor. So now she wasn't giving anything. Eventually she cried herself to sleep. That episode or as I call it the Baby Temptation Tantrum had me trying to figure out why this child went to such length of wanting something that bad that she did not know anything about. Later in life God revealed it to me that from a child we are curious about the unknown, building this way of selfishness, barely can talk but yet developed a way of using the term Mine...Mine... Mine. Even to a point were most starts out using the word NO (Negative) to certain extend before started using the word YES (Positive) depending on the situation at hand. As a child we'll start out loving things that's not ours, forming bad habits and learning bad ways. Again we have to pray over our children daily. These are souls that's being born. Born in the ways of sin. Unfortunately many of our children were taken away before they even realize that they were born. The devil is out there and he is doing his job everyday. We need to be praying daily trusting in God and putting God first in our lives. Jesus died for us so we can live. Without God in your life and accepting Jesus Christ as your Lord and Savior, you are that target, that child that don't know any better and still walking around saying mine...mine...mine. Seeking that unfamiliar spirit that will have you walking around as a time bomb. When do one grows out of this Baby Temptation Tantrum phase. Seeking, lusting and reaching out for that unfamiliar spirit and knowing full well that The spirit of God is right in front of you. Awaiting to give you that nurturing milk that will satisfy your spirit all the days of your life. Yet if one continues to not believe and seek from it's own selfish heart, trust and believe that the devour is awaiting to steal the mind, destroy the body and eventually kill your soul.

# Chapter 3

## THE POWER OF GOD'S LOVE

There was a time when God saw the act of the people and how it was filled with lust and corruption. Engaging in all types of sinful acts and the evil that dwelled in the imagination of mankind. He allowed it to rain for forty day and forty night. Wiping out all of mankind except for his chosen people, clean and unclean beasts and the fowls of the air, male and female to keep seed alive upon the face of the earth. As God saw fit and placed mankind back on land he blessed them and said "Be fruitful multiple and replenish the earth". God has spoken to his people, made himself known, performed miracles, from generation to generation but yet many still denied him and chose not to trust and obey his will. Whereas many seek to serve other gods leading up to facing destruction and demolishing. Not giving up on his people and because the loving God that he is, he sent his only begotten son to save the world. And again not only did mankind denied him they crucified him. Jesus sacrificed his body shed his blood for the love of God's people and to save mankind. So I ask, why many still denies him chose not to trust and obey the will of God.

JOHN 3:16

For God so loved the world, that he gave his only begotten Son, that whosoever believeth in him should not perish, but have everlasting life.

How is it that God who is the creator, breathe life into our lungs, love and protect us, bless us each and everyday but many hearts still stands harden. When life is good for them they praising and thanking him and yet when life storms comes at them they cussing and swearing under that same breath. God never said life is NOT going to bring forth storms it's how one stands on faith and trust in him when those storms come.

We are living in the last days. Look around people, even though the storms that's just beginning and will continue but it doesn't mean we cannot have heaven right here on earth. Success, peace, love, joy and happiness, wisdom and knowledge these things was granted and giving to us through his holy spirit. I can't speak for others but I can speak for myself. I can now look in the mirror and I like what I see. Like so many others I didn't always like that person that I saw looking back at me. It took me a long time to figure out who is this person and why is she even here. I had to cry out to my Lord and all I kept saying was why...why...why. Fifty plus years later I can look into that mirror, throw my hands up and say, thank you...thank you...thank you. The peace that he put upon me and in my life, sometimes feels like I am not even in this world. His presence in my soul at times has me feeling in perfect peace and his love that shields on me it's like I am not in my own body. I now know that my body don't have to die to be at peace and to be able to enjoy peace right here on earth. When I finally set aside all these things of the world, giving some family and friends over to him, shutting down enemies and negative energy that was trying to block God's blessings that he have for me, the new Kimberlyn has been born. I thank you Jesus for the renewal of my mind and my heart. Old things has passed away and behold all things are becoming new. As in your word, I have giving it all back to you. I am born again now I am a new creature in Christ. I am fearful and wonderfully made. I can do all things through Christ who strength me and I walk by faith and not by sight. I can now say, I Love Me and what all has become of me. I walk in the spirit and I am made one with The Father The Son and The Holy Spirit...Amen

There was a time in my life that I didn't always feel that peace nor did I walked in a Godly way. Starting out as a young Christian I knew God and his word but I had decided at times to do things my way. Good bad or indifference I still choose to make these decisions. Over the years there were times that I have paid for my mistakes, lost a lot but I've also learned a great deal and matured from it. There are times that I wish I can turn back the hands of time and have done things different. But thank God now that I know better I can do better. I definitely believe that God speaks to us at some means of signs, in our spirit or through someone else. The Holy Spirit will let us know how to walk with God. All you have to do is ask and you shall receive.

MATTHEW 7:7

Ask, and it shall be given to you; seek, and ye shall find, knock, and it shall be opened unto you.

WE HAVE TO LINE OUR SPIRIT UP IN THE SPIRIT OF GOD.

I can recall being in three fire episodes in my lifetime that almost took my life. One of the incident I pretty much was warned but again chose to do it my way. At the age of 18, I was about to graduate from High School, my class went on a senior trip to Great Adventures. At that time they had a fun house called The Haunted Castle. My friends and I decided to go into this Castle. Right away I felt this strange feeling come across me like it was saying not to go in. As I watch all the others people go in and out laughing and enjoying themselves, I decided to go in. As I started to go in that same feeling became stronger as if it was saying, not to go in. When I did go in at first it was that thrilling and suspense of not knowing what to expect. As part of the routine of this Haunted House you have scary imitated monsters and creatures coming at you, touching and making scary noise. A few friends and I cling to each other enjoying the moment and trying to make our way through this maze. All of a sudden I saw this bright light flicking and then getting brighter and stronger. There were this intense smell that started choking us. Now I realizing that there was actually a fire. The smell gotten stronger and the fire started spreading and becoming uncontrollable. I am now hearing people screaming, choking and crying for dear life. I went into a shock and just stood there because I knew at that time my life was over. But hearing this voice that kept saying come on...come on. Finally I started running. I didn't know where I was running to because it was pitch dark full of smoke and people running over each other. It seems like forever but finally I saw a bright light and not knowing if this light was going to be the light of life or death; I just ran towards it. Well that light was leading to the outside of this house and later I realized that the light was that light of life. When I made it outside I looked back and that entire house was in goofed in flames. I watch in horror knowing that there were still people trapped inside and watch those still coming out barely breathing. As we were shove on the school bus I've watch traumatized as this Castle burning down. Later it was reported that as of May 11, 1984 many High School students went out on a school trip to Great Adventure Amusement park in New Jersey and a Massive fire broke out in a fun house called The Haunted Castle. It killed 8 students leaving many students and The Park Attendants suffering from smoke inhalation.

When I looked back on this incident it wasn't so much of being trapped in the fire and survived it, it was more astonished of hearing the voice of God. Even in the midst of an disobedient act he love me and saved me. Writing this book based on Spiritually awakening has opened up the windows of my Soul and allow me to see that I could have been burned and buried in my own sin, but yet he kept me. Thirty plus years later I can testify, giving people hope that even at that moment when you feel like giving up because something went wrong. When that fire comes at you sometimes from that disobedient act and there is no possible way you think you are going to make it through, remember whatever situation you are in we serve a awesome God. The almighty heavenly father and there is nothing impossible for God. When you open up the windows of your soul, have that one to one relationship with him. Seek out his voice, be obedient to his calling so when that unfamiliar voice call for you (and it's going to call out for you) to do what God forbid you not to do, you won't get trapped in that fire. If you look around unfortunately not many escaped from that fire of life. When you continues to play with whatever fire that will come in your life, eventually you will get burned. Be hungry for God's word, seek his face and give your life to him then one will know and enjoy The Power of God's Love.

## EPHESIANS 6:11-13

(11) Put on the whole armour of God that ye may be able to stand against the wiles of the Devil.

(12) For we wrestle not against flesh and blood, but against principalities, against powers, against the rulers of the darkness of this world, against spiritual wickedness in high places.

(13) Wherefore take unto you the whole armour of God, that ye may be able to withstand in the evil day, and having done all, to stand.

Not being much of a out spoken person but more of a listener and observer, I have watched and studied certain behaviors of people because it pushes me more to pray for those who are lost, confused or don't know how to pray for themselves. So many people plays Russian-Roulette with their lives and don't really realize that they are doing it. And then there are some that takes such higher risk as if they have another chance on perishing then be reborn and reliving life again. Life can be hard because we choose to make it hard. I know because the Lord allows me to speak to many of his people, letting them know how powerful prayer is and how prayer does work if you believe. But understand that prayer and faith works together hand and hand. It's like describing a vehicle, there is that beautiful expensive car but without the engine that vehicle is worth nothing. It has to go hand and hand to make it complete. Having one shoe on and not having the other one on definitely makes your walking ability incomplete. When man/woman that tries to live on his/her own Island thinking that they don't need anybody, here is a little spiritual awakening, that's not God purpose for any individual. No man/woman cannot stand only. That's why God took woman from the rib of a man to stand together and to take that spouse as their own under the covenant of God, help making mankind complete. So the power of faith without works not only makes ones life incomplete it's actually dead. So when you pray, stand on faith and believe that whatever your heart desires under the will of God, it shall come to pass.

## MATTHEW 21:22

(21) Jesus answered and said unto them, Verily I say unto you, If ye have faith, and doubt not, ye shall not only do this which is done to the fig tree, but also if ye shall say unto this mountain, Be thou cast into the sea; it shall be done

(22) And all things, whatever ye shall ask in prayer, believing, ye shall receive.

STAND ON FAITH, TRUST AND BELIEVE AND WHEN YOU PRAY KNOW THAT ALL THINGS ARE POSSIBLE.

What makes prayer seems impossible is when you contradict yourself and trying to use God's words to satisfy your own selfish needs. Again observing and listening to people I notice that there are a whole lot of; God I need, I want, Can you, I will do that if you do this for me. I even came across those who use the power of God's words and try to use it against others. People what kind of God do you think we serve. Do you think we created him and he not created us. Let's not get it twisted. Be careful on who you ask to pray for you and what you are praying for because the devil can give you false answers to your prayers. Understand that whoever you line your Spirit up with (The Spirit of God or The spirit of the devil) that's where your prayer shall lay. If you don't know what to pray for or how to pray, ask the heavenly father and he will show you the way. Remember God is a spirit and lining up your spirit with the Spirit of God brings us under one accord. Praying to God is like having that one on one conversation with him. He knows our needs, our wants, pretty much every move we are about to make and everything we do. But just like you sit down and have that conversation with a love one, with that friend; we serve a loving God and he wants to have that conversation with us. To be technical not only do he hears us, it's he that changes things. Cast down mountains for us and can do all things that man/woman can't do. It's good to have conversation with one another that what God design for us to do, having that fellowship. But don't put all your trust in man/woman because we are human and humans make mistakes. Some of us means well but what it balls down to man woman child animal material things title money hell even statues do not have a heaven or hell to put us in. "God said give it all to me" Let's have more of a conversation with him. Let's praise him, giving him thanks and supplication. Listen to the voice of God and become more obedient to the spirit. Love him for just who he is and let's not underestimate the Power of prayer. God do answers prayers. Let us pray more and complain less.

We cannot want changes in our lives, looking for a perfect love that peace and happiness if we keep subjecting ourselves to constant drama and a negative lifestyle. Repeatedly introducing drama in our lives and under the same breath complaining that we don't want the drama. If we have a past, which we all do, then that's what it is and need to stay; in the past. If we are fortunate enough to come out a negative situation or negative environment, then leave it there and not return back and engage in that same lifestyle again. Don't let yourself get caught up in that negative spiritual realm because that negative energy will cling to you. It's not enough to be wrapped up in your own drama but other people drama to. That negative energy can be contagious and also addictive. When that seed is planted in your spirit, it will have you looking for more. I see so many people like to watch certain programs on television that contains so much drama and they get so caught up in it, they can't wait until the next episode comes on. The fighting, cussing, hatred and betrayal, deceit and seduction, people are feeding into it and so adamant about it that it's becoming apart of there lives. You even have those who seeks out for destruction. That's why it is so important to select your friends even certain family members into your circle. But then you have those who some how find themselves caught up in a situation and try so hard to remove this drama or uncomfortable situation from there lives. Yes it may be difficult and seems down right impossible, but I say anything is possible especially when you stand on faith. Again when you find God's favor and get delivered from negative spirits and energy, it's like crossing over to the other side of the street. From failure to success in a short distance it's like you taken that step from one corner to the next and doing so stay on that side, that's what helps makes the impossible possible.

As a child growing up I did not come from a strong spiritual background. Actually I didn't know much about God. I was taught to be strong minded, independent, respectful and fight for what I believed in. But looking around at so much negativity and lose souls it was hard to distinguish between right and wrong, not knowing what to believe in. Becoming a young woman I knew that the way of the world wasn't right and there had to be more to life than violence, hardship or just struggling to survive. I started out at a young age with trust issues and at one point in my life I've builded a wall that I felt to protect my heart and my mind from a hatred, deceitful and a cold hearted world. This caused me to walk this life not showing much love to anyone. Inspite of these feelings that was in my mind, my soul was crying out, starving to give love and to be loved. Not knowing where to turn and who to turn to. I heard this voice from deep inside of me but yet so clear as if it was coming out of my own mouth. I did not know then but the Holy Spirit revealed it to me later; that voice was the voice of God. Once I became born again baptized and saved at the age of 20 I was awaken to the whole meaning and purpose of life. God blessed me with a daughter followed by two sons that allowed to open my heart to love unconditionally and having the means of belonging to someone; and in my case belonging to my children. I've learned over the years what a mother has to do to sacrifice for her children and make touch decisions that will cause people to judge and try to throw stones at me. Even had a love one at that time try his best to break me and destroy my spirit. He knew using my children would be the only way that can break me but the harder he fought the more I cried out to the Lord. When God stepped in the devil couldn't no longer touch me. I did what people did not expected. After been called so many unpleasant names, talked about, laughed at and unfortunately being wished the worst on, I still loved and pray for that person. This is when I knew that love can conquer and break any unholy spirit. When that spiritual war was over and it almost cause the life of that individual. I prayed harder stand on faith and trust in the Lord with all my soul. Through the grace of God he spared his life. Even when a second chance was giving he will still try to strike out to destroy me all because in his mind it was his way of... "Loving me". I am ever so grateful that I was delivered and knew the difference between walking in the love of God and walking in the way of the world. Coming to that understanding I had experienced over the years different ways on how people called themselves loving me. The more I seek the love of God and to show Godly love to others the more the enemy tried to keep doubt in my heart. By means of abuse, mistreatment, accusing, lying and so much more that kept coming into my life from those that claimed again that they "Love me". Never giving up, walking by faith and not by sight and believing in God's love. Beside the unconditionally love of my Children I thank God for the love of his living angels that he placed in my life. Being blessed and loved by them helped kept me rooted and grounded, strong and disciplined, hungry but yet full in the word of God. Thank you Pastor Ernest Cameron and Pastor Barbara Cameron. As a young woman in my twenties to be introduced and feed the word of God. Nurtured my spirit and help showed me the way on how to love…God's Love. Diane Person Santiago not only was she my best friend but my Spiritual Mom loving me like her own child. She supported me and believed in me. We laughed and cried together, from the countless hours of our conversations every time we talk on the phone to relaxing in the house and talking for hours throughout the years. She became like my mom after the Lord called my biological mother home. She too went home to be with the Lord. Both of my moms was the strongest women I ever known and molded me to be the strong and God-fearing woman that I am today. Right when I thought that the blessings stop there, Pastor Samuel Johnson and Mother Julanne Renee Johnson stepped into my life as to my cup becoming so full from the love they showered me with. Their Godly walk, their strength, faith and humbleness that embedded into my life. I have learned and experienced so much and I am so grateful for God using such a loving and loyal couple to show me what true love is and the meaning of marriage. Mother Johnson being my best friend/spiritual mom and Godmother I can't express the love I have for you. Mother thank you and know that I love you and Pastor from every square inch of my heart. To my Mother and Father Bessie Mae and Gerald Leader if I had that one last wish to see your face again. Your was my greatest inspiration and I am so proud to be the continuation of your vessel and blood line as a Leader. Like so many others unfortunately wait until the passing of our parent(s) look back and say...I wish I was there more, helped out or just simply say...I love you. Right now hopefully until we meet again Mom and Dad sleep in peace and I will forever give thanks and love to you both. As my love and faith has grown for others, I cannot express the respect, thanks and love for our formal 44th President of the United States Barack Obama and 1st lady Michelle Obama. If we just sit back and let it register in our souls that this making of History is a lifetime change to the opening of windows for our next generation. We had many powerful Black people that stood up believing in the people, fought for the people and unfortunately died to make a difference for the people. Barack Obama wasn't just a movement that just happened nor was he this black man that came in and out of this White House just to make a few changes and brought forth a Voice that came and went. His walk in life, his love for his family and the people, his dreams, loyalty, commitment and faith that has awaken so many souls that had many unbelievers stand up and say "There is a God". Barak and Michelle Obama has helped bring my faith up to the top of the scale. When I didn't have much faith in myself such as being able to write a book more or less having my voice stand out through this book and hopefully being heard to make a difference in many lives. When I looked back on that moment that had me in tears, when Obama took his wife by the hand, step out that vehicle and walked proudly and with great faith, through the multiple crowd of people on that Victory day as President of the United States. Looking back unfortunately President John F. Kennedy did not make it through as the devil stepped in using a soul(s) to take his life away. Inspite of, Obama walked on faith and as that inspired me, my walk is stronger as I walk by Faith and not by Sight. I ask you, what stumbling block that's there in your life that is keeping you from reaching your full potential. Let's try what you think is impossible and let's make it possible. Step out of that vehicle, hold on tho the hands of our Lord and savior Jesus Christ and walk through that crowd with boldness, love and strength. As you hold your head up to thy Heavenly Father walk by faith and not by sight and feel the Power of God's love. Like Obama, you too can walk through that crowd with great victory and success. Accept God's blessings, allowing his will to be done in your life. I, myself, now believe in true love and accept the greatest love that's there... GOD'S LOVE.

# Chapter 4

# BUILDING A FOUNDATION

## ROMANS 8:28

We know that all things works together for good for those who love God, to those who are called according to his purpose.

WE HAVE THE POWER TO OVERCOME AND TAKE CONTROL OVER OUR LIVES.

When you are building something normally it starts with an foundation. So if one decides to build a house he/she needs to start from the base line, making sure it is solid and firm to hold whatever that's placed on it. In my case I love growing plants and when I start with the foundation or the seed(s) I will examine and nurture it. Making sure it gets everything it needs to help it mature blossom and develop into a beautiful, strong and attractive plant. Many of us has this talent to create something starting from the foundation, building on it and creating this masterpiece. Spending countless hours, investing in large amount of money and not even counting the energy, loyalty and love of it to get it exactly the way they want it...PERFECT.

Thank God for those that have that God gifted talent that helped build and turned our nation so great. Building up our Landmarks bridges and beautiful historical places. Either getting paid for it or just enjoying what they can do, they made it happened. From the beginning of time God created the heaven and the earth, from Noah building The Noah's Ark to now when Mankind builded up this beautiful Nation that we live in. It was destined by the power of God to bring forth the beauty of our Country. From Country to Country, State to State, City to City the phenomenal creation that was built to make the United States of America to such greatness. The Water Falls in Niagara Falls, The Eiffel Tower in Paris, the building of The World Trade Center in New York City, this creation was done by the power of God giving unto Mankind. To my surprise I have known people who was fortunate enough to have visited these places and yet found means of complaints or just wasn't pleased. Ok I get it, you can't please everybody. But I have learned to get a better understanding of people. We have such greatness of places or a place that feels like heaven here on earth, making our world a place of comfort and peace until some returns to their permanent place of home in Heaven. A place where he has many Mansions, where there is no pain or suffering, no tears or fear and no more hatred and evildoers but to live everlasting life with the heavenly Father and being one with our Lord and Savior Jesus Christ. Yet these places which was designed and build, beautified and attractive, satisfying comfortable and enjoyable to the people and still there are so many of those that find means of dissatisfaction and complaints. If we have those who sees ugliness in such greatness, imagine what they see in just good. It allows me to get a better picture and pray for those who wakes up in good health, fine homes and cars, a nice size bank account and or have traveled to places that only many have dreamed of; and yet complains the most and still not satisfied. The more that's giving to them the more they want. Claiming what's rightfully belong to others and/or wants to be giving credit for something that they did not do. We are blessed and giving so much and yet these people lust over these worldly things; Being beyond greed. It is known to be said that money is the root of evil. I've always wanted to clarify that. It's not the money which is nothing but paper, it's the hands that control this paper. The power that one feels when they have so much more than others; use and manipulate those that's are less fortunate. Yes, we do need money for survival and to create a good lifestyle for ourselves but at the same time one needs to control the money and not let the money control them. Just like you have good and evil, money can go either way. Now there are some that's are living a very comfortable lifestyle and enjoying all the fine things of life and are in the need for nothing. Having just about everything they want. In good spirit they have taken some of that fortune and gave back to the communities, help provided the need for the less fortunate people and/or donated to charity; giving others or someone a better lifestyle. Then you have those living angels touched by God that gives away just about all that they have to the unfortunate. On the other hand you have those who sells their souls to the Devil. Using their riches and fortune to take down others in the means of destruction. Now when you have those who lust or love over money and do evil doing toward others, well let's shake this up a little with some knowledge, those things which are of the world stays in this world. It's just temporary and you will not be taking it with you to wherever your place of permanent residence is going to be. When the gates of heaven opens up it's far much more then one can imagine and to enter into such an extraordinary and phenomenal place of infinity leaves ones Soul at rest. The greatest price that one has pay is actually FREE. So that same dollar bills that one holds so tightly is not going to buy your way into heaven. This is why the devil try so hard to capture as many souls as he can to gain power in keeping souls captivated and tormented for the place of hell and one of the ways of doing this so is through the lust of money.

## MATTHEW 16:26

(26) For what is a man profited, if he shall gain the whole world, and lose his own soul? Or what shall a man give in exchange for his soul?

So this misconception that money is the root of evil blinds our people of the truth. That why it is so important when praying, ask God for wisdom and knowledge. The power that mankind gain from the control of money can either be a blessing for that person or to someone else. On the negative side it can be use for the means of destruction.

You probably feel me by now on how I like to take it back to the beginning, to the hard core roots to where it all began.

## GENESIS 1:26

(26) And let them have dominion over the fish of the sea, and over the cattle, and over all the earth.

People why go to the devil to get what's already ours. God already give us all the things of the earth. As much is giving as much is received. We have to work for it, claim what's ours and thank God for it. People why kill yourselves, hurt others and try to destroy what God has given us and it's right there all along in our face for mankind to be at peace and enjoy. Again as much is giving as much is received. We know that the devil came to Jesus three times trying to tempt his.

## MATTHEW 4:9-10

(9)The devil spoke to Jesus and said "All these things will I give thee, if thou wilt fall down and worship me".

(10)Now Jesus did reply by saying "Get there hence, Satan: for it is written, Thou shalt worship the Lord thy God, and him only shalt thou serve. Now when I got knowledge of this, I referred back to Scripture.

John 1:3. All things were made by him; and without him was not anything made that was made.

So how can the lying Devil try to give Jesus what is already his. We are inheritance of Jesus Christ, these things was already giving to us and plenty of. Even from the talent that God gave us in building up our Counties to the gift of Gold, Silver, Oil, Money, etc…, God said all these things I give until mankind; for God's purpose. So people are taking what they inherent already, allowing the devil to manipulate them to misuse, mistreat, rob steal kill and destroy each other to gain control, power and respect. In all my days I've been trying to put two and two together and I keep coming up with twenty two instead of four. Only because what appears to be simply we make it so difficult. Again I say that we have the power and control over our own lives and what we make of it is how we live. Good bad or indifference when our number is called and when it's all over, there is only one person who we are going to answer to and face on the day of judgment. God's will…will be done.

I speak out loud and clear that we the people can lose this battle of life because we are losing sight of the only thing that can stop this War…PRAYER. When one stop believing, lose trust and faith in the power of God, there is nothing left but the grain of sand that's ready to be washed away when that tide comes at anytime. PRAYER is that rock that cannot be moved. PRAYER is what makes the impossible possible. PRAYER is what God hears and he and only he can turn this losing battle of life to an winning victory, but it starts and end with the power of prayer. Trust and believe prayer does work.

# Chapter 5

# THE POWER OF THE TONGUE

Through the Spirit of God we are made in the perfect will of our Heavenly Father. Being under one accord with our Lord and Savior Jesus Christ. Manifested in a body in the perfect will of God. Knowing that we are made up of living organs that has its own functions but yet works together under one accord; placed in a body that gives us means of life. But that one particular organ that not only does it help produce life but it can also bring forth death and that's the Power of the Tongue.

### PROVERBS 18:21

Death and Life are in the power of the tongue: and they that love it shall eat the fruit thereof.

Many people don't really understand how powerful the tongue can be. Giving this gift from God to be able to speak but what we speak about or confess out of our mouth can either bring forth a blessing or destruction in one's life and/or someone else's life. We have heard the saying, "Be careful what you ask for because you just might get what you asked ". I think we all have been there as far as praying and asking for something, someone, somewhere different or just some type of change in our lives. Then there are times when we receive it we wish that we never asked for it. Being placed in a bad situation under anger or hurt toward someone we tend to say negative and/or profound words to that person.

Sometimes wishing sickness and pain toward them. Just to name a few hatred words that's many of us has confessed out of our mouth. I wish that you will drop dead, I pray that you will go to hell, I hate you, I wish that you were never born, and the list goes on and on. Unfortunately it seems like the ones that we are closest to are the one that we tend to confessed hatred toward. Under the same breath we can tell a person how much we love them and then turn around cold hearted telling them how much we hate them. Now you have those that I call "Sharp Edge Hate-Lovers". They so call tell you how much they love you but on the other hand the words that they confess out of their mouths, it's like a two-edge sword piercing through one's heart. The sad part about it, we choose these negative words using it against a person/people that can really cause damage in their walk of life and sometimes they can have a hard time bouncing back from it. You can push them away causing them to distance themselves from you but God forbid tragedy strike and they pass away. I have seen it over and over again...the blamed and guilt that strips that persons soul to a point where their lives is no longer the same. So many people have giving up on their own lives because it becomes too difficult for them to bare. Whereas those that walks around in a numb state of mind trying to bury their feelings in alcohol drug depression and to some degree have committed suicide. Without really realizing it we have use negative words against ourselves allowing negative energy to manifest in our lives. I am fat, I can't do it, I am never going to be successful, I wish I was dead; do any of this sounds familiar. I can tell you what God say about this.

## EPHESIANS 4:29

Let no corrupt communication proceed out of your mouth, but that which is good to the use of edifying, that it may minister grace unto the hearers.

That's why it is so important that we guard our hearts. I have mention in a earlier chapter, what we feed our spirit will manifest in our hearts and we will confess it out of our mouths. Please here me people...What one speak through the power of the tongue that is held by the beat of the heart can either bring forth destruction or life. As one will say; we all need a wake up call. But as it is written, we all need a Spiritual Awakening.

We need to speak life into our lives. Over each other and our children lives. Come on God's children, let's get away from feeding our spirit in these dramatized television shows and being able to communicate without using cursing and profound language to express ourselves. Let's not poison our children minds and corrupt their spirit in this Social Media World and negative dramatized reality shows. Not good for nothing but what you find cute when this child acts out, laugh when they say something bad or even giving in to them when they want their way, you are going to reap what you sow. Again I love taking it back to the hard core roots, in the beginning where it all begins. Take time out listen to your children and give respect when respect is due and it will be given back to you. Walk with grace and love, like little hens our children will walk in the same path right behind you. Be a Leader and not a follower. Know who you are and your purpose as a child of God. By nature our children feed from our vibes, study and learn what is projected to them. Let's walk as Conquerors, Kings and Queens, Warriors and

Ministers of God. Let's take back what's rightfully ours. Walk in Love and make your life and your children lives the way God intended it to be. LETS NOT BE OUR OWN WORST ENEMIES. I believe through the power of the tongue when we speak life over our own lives our days will be longer. Let's not give the enemy any place in your heart; guard it, protect it and make room for whatever blessings that God has in-store for you. That blessings just might be a blessing to others. Sometimes it can be harder and takes longer for some because of negativity and anger that was built up for so long in their mind and/or in their heart. But when you give it to God and set your circle around positive people, positive energy, you will find yourself doing positive things not only for yourself but others as well. Then will you find a peaceful and happier lifestyle as well as confessing and speaking with love. Now you may have those that will say, Kim what world are you living in. I will stand bold and proudly and say, Try it you just might like it.

# Chapter 6

## THE SEED OF LIFE

I found that the human brain is also another powerful and fascinating organ that makes us who we are. This soft convoluted mass of gray and white matter serves control and coordinate the mental and physical action. As part of my profession in the medical field I had to take up and study Anatomy and Physiology and during my studies I found the brain to be one of the most fascinating and interesting organ. Observing of the brain on how it's formed and it's functions helps me to understand more so the power of God. Out of a seed creates life forming a body and placed all aspect of living organs perfectly function together under one accord. Giving an extension of the head that holds and protect the brain which protrude the mind that controls the body and it all coming together through the holy spirit; creating the meaning of life. We know that the brain is made up of nerve cells which interact with the rest of the body through the spinal cord and nervous system. The ability to move, speak, comprehend, the controlling of one's feelings, all controlled by the brain. If the brain is not functioning properly all kinds of damage can be done to other organs and it's functions. I like to view the brain as the leak to the chain. As everything connect altogether in the body the leak (brain) holds it altogether and this what brings forth the meaning of Life. The SEED where life begins. We have to understand how important the brain or mind is that's started from a seed that brings forth life to make us who we are. If a good seed is planted it will bring for goodness and if a bad seed is planted therefore badness or corruption will it produce. What I find to be so disturbing is when a child is born and starts become observing and inquisitive where as they start putting things in their mouths or touch things, the first thing some parent(s) will say is he/she is bad. Even to the point of telling the child over and over again... "You are bad" "You don't listen". Are you not realizing that you are already feeding this negative energy into the child spirit/ mind. Not only do that parent(s) or a caregiver for the child speaks all types of negativity but projects all types of negative behavior around or to the child/children. Already bringing forth corruption into the child(s) mind. Let's take it back to the beginning. Again I love starting from the beginning. That's where you'll find the answer to most of the problems that we are facing today. We know that God intended for us to be fruitful and multiple. Bringing forth life and as God breathed life into our living soul, we are intended to be born under the perfect will of God. As I mention early we were created through the Holy Spirit in the image of our Father God and through our Lord and Savior Jesus Christ. So to be one with God our daily walk should be lined up with the will of God renewing our mind every day.

## ROMANS 12:2

(2) Be not conformed to this world: but be ye transformed by the renewing of your mind, that ye may prove what is that good, and acceptable, and perfect will of God.

To be born under the means of a corrupted mind, the mind projects negative thoughts and now acting on negative energy. As a child or your own child watching hearing disfunctional behaviors this act continues to repeats from generation to generation. Let me give you a little bit of a spiritually awaken. This is why it's so important to pray and renew your mind daily. We have the power to help bring forth positive God-fearing loving souls into the world. It is so essential when praying to believe in the power of God and stand on faith as that seed is planted before life even begins. When a man and woman decides to come together to interact or engage in sexual activities especially when not using any means of protection, the chances of producing a child is high. We always have spirit(s) watching us. Remember God sees everything and the devil enjoy watching also. If or when this act is performed depending on where your spirit laid more likely that will be the results you will get from the seed that is planted. Either a corrupted or uncorrupted seed life will began.

The strongest bond that there is, is the bond between husband and wife. Together mix with faith, the love of God (putting God first in their lives) and walking together in obedience with the Lord, no weapon shall form against them and prosper and if any mountains comes against them it will be cast down and removed. In the name of Jesus, whatsoever they pray for they shall receive.

MARK 11:23-24

(23) For verily I say unto you, That whosoever shall say unto this mountain, Be thou removed, and be cast into the sea; and shall not doubt in his heart, but shall believe that those things which he saith shall come to pass; he shall have whatsoever he saith.

(24) Therefore I say unto you, What things so ever he desire, when he pray, believe that ye receive them, and he shall have them.

When two people bonded together under one spirit being fruitful and multiple bringing forth Life, bearing children is intended to brings forth a uncorrupted seed. Through prayer and faith bless will be that child and generations to come. But those who submit to other spirits being out of the will of God, enjoying the fruit of their own lust, brings forth a corrupted seed, bearing children, curse will be that child and that generations to come. When there's no bond there's no connection. So things starts to scattered around making it easy for everything to get lost. But when you have that bond (like the husband and his wife) things stands strong firm and together only if you believe.

As the world will say, The mind is a terrible thing to waste. This is one of the reasons why I find the brain to be so fascinating because of the power of the mind. Either it can be against you or for you.

## II CORINTHIANS 10:5

Casting down imagination, and every high things that exalt itself against the knowledge of God, and bringing into captivity every thought to the obedience.

As it is written, without knowledge and wisdom one will perish. I found the key that helps me to obtain such wisdom and knowledge is becoming more of a listener and less of a speaker. Listening and watching people more so in today's time complaining, depressed, angry, confused, full of hatred, ready to give up or already gave up more so then ever. Living out of the will of God this is going to happen. When you have those who proudly walks around saying this is my common law husband or wife (Law that was made by man), or my baby daddy, my babies momma but not many saying, this is my husband or my wife. Those who walks around with this, It's all about me and my way, state of mine (Again out of the will of God). Men with men, Women with women or decides to take on the gender of the opposite sex, again out of the will of God. Adults and parents that are losing control over their children and when it becomes out of control, now watching them trying to gain that power back is like a mockery toward that parent(s). Seeing how some kids finding it to be a joke and/or enjoying satisfaction of watching their parent(s) being at risk of serving jail time. Worst yet that parent that don't know how to gain the proper control or power and end up causing serious damage or even death to that child/children. All this to say mankind brings on destruction to themselves to their love ones because they walk as their own god or corrupted gods. Anything that stands out of the will of the Heavenly Father has no foundation and eventually it will fall.

# Chapter 7

## UNFORGIVENESS

What I find to be the most hardest and challenging thing for most people to encounter is unforgiveness. If one have lived then you have been there one way or another; not forgiving that someone or others that hurt, caused harm or flick pain in your life. By choice so many has chooses to never forgive and then there are many that has died and taken that unforgiveness to their grave. Whereas some still struggle trying hard to release that unforgiving energy that has builded up to a point that, that pain is embedded down into their soul. That's why we need to come to terms and understand the seriousness of living life with an unforgiving heart. Knowing how that heavy baggage and poisonous energy not only affect the mind and heart but also causes physical changes in the body. Mentally when that negative energy takes control over ones heart and captivating their mind that seriousness is known to cause that person to live their life under this spirit of darkness and anger. This chronic anger can put you into a fight-or-flight mode, which result in numerous changes in heart rate, blood pressure and immune response. Those changes, then, increase the risk of depression, heart disease and diabetes, among other health conditions. Stress is known to be one of the leading causes that contributes to heart attacks or even death. Again we need to understand the intense amount of stress that is put on those who walks around with a harden heart and with that spirit of unforgiveness. That unforgiving spirit is more likely to do more damage to the person that's holding on to that energy than the person/people that's actually caused or causing the damage. As I made mention in the previous chapter how powerful the brain is in controlling the mind, the heart is just as powerful in controlling of the body. Let's not give anyone that much power over you and let's take a good look behind the scene (one's heart). God give us a free will and we have the power and control to what we allow and except in our space, mind and heart. Unfortunately there are so many depraver and vicious individuals that seek out to prey one's mind, finding satisfaction and pleasure on flicking pain to another. The disturbing thing about it, more than most, it's against a love one or close friend. The power behind this that can break this negative energy is positive energy. When one wants to throw hate at you throw back that love, step back and watch how that whole vibe changes in your favor. Then look back again behind that same scene (one's heart) and see how that situation will work out in a way that will have your heart singing and your mind at peace. In the natural being one can not do this by themselves, that negative energy has its place of power. We have to bring in the power of the holy spirit because at hand we are facing a spiritual warfare. This is why we are giving a comforter; to protect, guide and lead us into a place of forgiveness and peace. The natural being will find it to difficult to forgive and have you walking away in the means of anger. We don't have to waste so much energy and time. The simplest thing we find to do we make it the hardest. Give it to God, call on Jesus and allow the holy spirit to do its job. Then will one find means to forgive that person or people that seeked out ways to hurt them. I find praying for those complicated souls and asking our heavenly Father to help them settle in their own ways. Many are so caught up in the devil's work they become lost in their own mind and may find themselves believing that what's wrong is right and what's right is wrong. Sometimes it's good to walk away from certain situation because unfortunately they just don't know any better.

Like myself I find that the holy spirit always brings me back to the word of God and that every situation at hand is in the hands of God.

## PSALM 109:1-4

(1) Hold not thy peace, O God of my praise;

(2) For the mouth of the wicked and the mouth of the deceitful are opened against me: they have spoken against me with a lying tongue.

(3) They compassed me about also with words of hatred; and fought against me without a cause.

(4) For my love they are my adversaries: but I give myself unto prayer.

What I find to be so astonished is the fact that so many of God's children knows "The Lord's Prayer" and many will quote it daily word from word. They would teach their children, they would confess it in and out of church, but still finds it difficult to live by it. Now because you may already know this prayer allow me to center out these verses:

## MATTHEW 6:12

(12) And forgive us our debts, as we forgive our debtors. Also allow me to make mention in:

## MATTHEW 6:14-15

(14) For if ye forgive men their trespasses, your heavenly Father will also forgive you:

(15) But if ye forgive not men their trespasses, neither will your Father forgive your trespasses.

So this well known simply but powerful prayer that's embedded in us, our children and our children's children, yet we asks of Heavenly Father to forgive us of our sins but we are not willing to forgive those who sinned and hurted us. Again as in the natural this can be one of the hardest and challenging things that we are facing because of pride, hurt, anger and other sources of negative energy that can cause mental, emotional or even physical damage on one's being. As you quote the Lord's Prayer and other prayers that the Holy Spirit may lead you to confess remember this fight is not our fight. However the enemy tries to comes at you remember you are never alone. Forgive in thou heart, cleanse your mind and walk in peace. Give it to God. Greater he that is in you then he that's in this world.

# Chapter 8

# JUDGEMENT

To be connected and listening to the voice of God is strengthening my spiritual walk as I grow and age gracefully. I have seen so much in my time, mature enough to now sit back and enjoy the peace that God places in my home, my heart and in my life. This allows me to help those in the need and pray for those who are lost. As many sit back and judge one another, I lifted them up prayer because we all fall short of the glory of God and to come to term that a sin is a sin. There is no one's sin greater than the next persons sin. Hearing people judging those who are committing adultery yet those same people who commits fornication finds it to be not a sinful act. (I have not yet figured that one out). Then you'll find others that commits adultery/fornication forming all types of sexual acts and bashing those who performs sexual acts with the same sex. (Still trying to figure that out). There is no less or greater sin. We all will get measured by the measure we meet.

MATTHEW 7:1-3

(1)Judge not, that ye be not judge

(2)For with what judgement ye judge, ye shall be judged: and with what measured ye mete, it shall be measured to you again.

(3)And why behold thou the mote that is in the brother's eye, but consider not the beam that is in this own eye?

I find this to be one of the most powerful message that God brought forth to his people that needs to be addressed over and over until maybe one day we can get it right. So if one not quite understanding it from this term let's try to bring forth this message from God in a different terminology. From the English Standard Version (ESV) Bible.

"Judge not, that you be not judged. For with the judgement you pronounce you will be judged, and with the measure you use it will be measured to you. Why do see the speck that is in your brother's eye, but do not notice the log that is in your own eye?.

Take note that as we examine our outer appearance in the mirror everyday, we need to practice examining our inner (Spiritual) self everyday. Maybe then you can bring forth improvement in the life of the one who is looking back at you in that mirror.

We tend to come across this assumption that one should know better so we start passing judgement. There are so many individuals that faces weakness mentally and even though they are aware of their wrong doing, their losing mental battle with themselves will drive them to become judgmental towards others. As there are so many who are struggling of making their own rightful life decision are the same ones who's trying to make decisions over someone else's unsettle life decision. Conjunction to those who gets involved in other people lives, watching them or being apart of their down fall. Finding satisfaction in either talk about them and/or judging the outcome of their life. But on the other hand when you have those who spends so much time and energy judging others not only are they losing out on their own blessings but it will contribute negative energy in their lives.

You find that hundreds, thousands of people come together marching, protesting and uniting together for many causes. To bring justice and protecting the rights of the people. Making changes to build up our communities, our schools, even fighting for more or better jobs for the people. These are some great causes and needs to continue being addressed until these needs are met. But what about fighting for our Churches. We talk about the problems in the Church and many even stay away from going to Church. Now we have so many different belief and each individual has the right to serve God in whatever belief or religion they committed to. However the way one serves God and worship him, it narrows down to we all serve the same God. The heavenly father that gave us life, that knew us before we was even in our mother's womb. That same God that created the Heaven and earth, the sun, the moon, the stars...etc., the same God that we all will stand and face on our day of judgement. But we still stand to face so many problems in the church and one of the major problems is Judging one and another. God said in his house pray for one another, edify and build up each other, not judging and tearing down one another. For he brought forth his only begotten son who is life and the light of this world and he came not to pass judgement but to save the world. So who are we to pass judgement. There was separation in the church from the beginning of time and it still stands today. But there is nothing impossible for God in the name of Jesus. Trust and believe just like the wall of Jericho came tumbling down after Joshua's Israelite army marched around the city blowing their trumpets. So just imagine the miracle and changes that will be made if we unite and bring hundreds of thousands or millions of people if not more, fighting to bring down those negative strong holds in God's house. To bind up the devil, his demonic spirits along with his followers in the church. You know those souls that sits in Church full of hatred, jealousy, greed, lies and deceit. The ones that smiles in your face but dressed in wolf clothing, trying to run souls out of the church. But through the power of prayer, praying in the spirit, walking by faith, Holy Ghost filled, standing on the blood of Jesus, We can stop the separation in the church, get rid of those unwanted spirits and win souls into Christ.

I know with no doubt that if God's people come together by the hundreds, thousands or better yet by the millions praying, trusting in God, walking with Jesus you won't believe how many souls that will be saved. Just knowing this brings forth the love, peace, unite of the people that is meant by the will of God. That chain will be broking where you have many that sits home saying I don't need to go to Church. I don't go to church because there are nothing but hypocrites there and Pastors/Ministers or Bishops that always seem to pass around the plates numerous of time taking all of my money. Then you'll have those that's saying, I don't need to go to church to pray and serve God because I can do it right from home. There is truth in that but again let me give you heads up on a some Spiritual Awakening.

### I JOHN 4:1-3

(1) Beloved, believe not every Spirit, but try the spirit whether they are of God: because many false prophets are gone out into the world.

(2) Hereby know ye the spirit of God. Every Spirit that confess that Jesus Christ is come in the flesh is of God.

(3)And every spirit that confess NOT that Jesus Christ is come in the flesh is NOT of God and this is that spirit of antichrist, whereof ye have heard that it should come; and even now already is it in the world.

You cannot take on these spirits in your natural works. We have to try the spirit so you will know if it is coming from God. Staying home and praying but know who you are praying to. Not trusting in giving back the ten percent of your tithes and offering, as well that same money that you are holding on to, was giving to you by the blessing of God in the first place. There are many spirits and without the Holy Spirit who are you praying to. Just like we have to be taught everything else, we also have to be taught how to prayer. Yes, there are false Prophets, Pastors, Ministers and Bishops out there which gives us more reasons to know how to pray and take back the house of God. Let's knock down those wall in the church with the Holy Spirit and take back what God rightfully have giving us; as we give back to him our tithes and offering. Take that leap of faith and not sit at home but in the house of God. If we can march protest and fight for everything else why not fight in the Spirit for the will of God.

# Chapter 9

## JESUS IS THE WAY

JOHN 14:6

I AM THE WAY, THE TRUTH, AND THE LIFE: NO MAN COMETH UNTO THE FATHER, BUT BY ME.

When you read the bible have you ever wonder who God was talking to when he said in GENESIS "Let's make man in OUR image". From beginning of time Jesus sat at the right hand of the father. All things that was made was made through him and by him; yet many denies him. He performed miracle through the power of the Heavenly Father; yet many denies him. He was wounded for our transgressions, bruised for our iniquities the chastisement of our peace and shed his blood to save mankind; yet many denies him. He even went to hell for us so we don't have to, again many still don't believe.

When I hear people talk of denial or unbelief about the Lord I stay far away. If they think that they can crucify Jesus again what more would they try to do to me and I wasn't the one who died for them. That same spirit of denial that dwells in so many from beginning of time to this day. You'll have mothers who set aside that good child but yet favors the child that gives her the most trouble. You will find many women that turns away from a good man but run behind those men that engaged in several women, don't do much for her and barely shows her any love or support, But yet she'll denies that good man for that misleading one. Whereas the same applies to the those men that will leave what's good at home. From the love, loyalty and respect that's giving to him, even as his rightful position as the man of the household, yet he will seek for as I call it; those mask wearing women. You know the ones I am talking about. Those women that dolls themselves up with beautiful makeup, false hair boobs butt nails whatever she can find to disguise herself and to lured a man in. These men that will gravitate towards these women sacrificing everything they build at home, losing that good women for again that mask wearing woman. That spirit of denial can be that persons down fall, from losing of a love one to everything they have. It's one thing to lose that love one or your possession but to lose out of your blessings or worst your salvation.

What I notice about people is you'll have those who talks as if they know everything and they can take on the world thinking they have all the answers. When things are going good in their life at that time they don't need Jesus. Feeling that since of satisfaction and money situation is good. They receiving all the material things that they need and want, even down to feeling loved by that special person/people in their life. So why call on Jesus or have any type of personal relationship with him. Life is good for them without the Lord. They would have him buried or tuck away for whatever means of safe keep for them. Now when life storm comes at them, they will be the one that you will hear calling on him. "Jesus...Jesus help me" "Lord I can't do this" but the best part is when they start to bargain with the him. "I promise to do this if you do that for me". "Give me one more chance and I promise I will change ". I heard it all. Now when things goes there way again all of that bargaining goes out the window. People understand, God said let your Yes be your Yes and your No be your No. You can't live your life being lukewarm nor live this life using the Lord for your purpose. Let's not get it twisted. You can not bury him and bring him back to life when things are not going your way or when you find yourself in a situation that you can not get out of. Now you want to pray when you are losing that love one or finding out that your own health is falling. I can understand that there are many that don't know any better but yet it's that person responsible to know. That's why it is so important to seek wisdom and knowledge because the lack of can determine where you will spend your eternity. You have to renew our minds everyday, shut down the flesh crucified with Jesus and walk in the spirit day by day.

## GALATIANS 2:20

I am crucified with Christ: Nevertheless I live; not I, but Christ liveth in me: and the life which I now live in the flesh I live by the faith of the son of God, who loved me, and gave himself for me.

It is one of the greatest thing to see people especially those who was held back because of the color of their skin, in school or went back to school. To receive that title that's now apart of their name, walking away with honors awards and special trophies. That feeling that he/she experience that no one can't take away from them. Feeling that means of success and achievement that they have accomplished especially through their times of struggles that made them who they are today. Being able to enjoy the fine things of life and to live comfortable. You had some that received that love and support from family and friends, then there are those that did not, but yet stands great leaving back a legacy and/or carried that torch for the next generation. It's good to give credit where credit is due but it best to give recognition and thanks to where it all comes from, Through the Grace of God; and to know that God supply all our needs according to his riches in glory by Christ Jesus.

## ROMANS 8:28

We know that all things work together for good to them that love God, to them who are called according to his purpose. God grace and mercy is upon his children. He loves us so that he gave us his only begotten son and through our Lord and savior we can do all things through Christ who strengthen us. CHILDREN OF GOD REMEMBER THAT THERE IS NOTHING BEFORE GOD'S TIME.

# Chapter 10

## AGAPE LOVE

From the moment some parent(s) sees their newborn for the first time or that loving pet that they decided to take home, they instantly falls in love. Then there are those moments when we lay eyes on that special person and our heart skips that beat, believing that he/she is the one, and we fall madly in love. There are some that have that best friend(s) that they love so dearly that they can't imagine living their lives without them or that selected person. Like myself some people love plants and love growing it in there homes or out in their gardens. Now there are those who have that, what I call, lusting love of money and/or of material things. Having the love for our family, friends, and the list goes on and on. So with all of that said what is this powerful force that we call Love and what is the real meaning of Love. How and why some people can love someone one minute and in the next minute can hate them. Then on the other hand some people can love so deeply that they have killed themselves or others behind this thing that's called...Love. So again I say what is this emotional energy, this force that can make people actions become good or bad. That can turn a person from an unsettle, irrational negative behavior to a calm caring positive behavior. On the other hand that same emotional energy can have an individual go from that positive behavior to a hatred and negative behavior; yet they will confess there love for someone. So how do one digest all this energy. The only way to find out is through the love of God because he is Love

# 1 JOHN 4:8 AND 12

(8) For God is Love.

(12) No man hath seen God at anytime. If we love one another, God dwell in us, and his love is perfect in us.

Without the love of God it is impossible to please God and to walk in that perfect kind of love. That perfect Love is God's Agape Love and when that love is broken that walk in love is taking over by this emotional energy known to be the Lust of Love. Mankind has been trying to take on this love without God but It's like trying to drive a car without the engine. See God is that engine and without that you are not going anywhere. Your life become a stand still that will have you feeling lost confused and lonely. When you start feeling lost without the love of God or God's Agape Love in your life that's when many tend to put on this mask. This mask that people will hide behind taking on these emotional feelings and acting according to the reputation of that mask. Now classified the meaning of their love however that's suitable for them. Basically our spiritual walk in love either it's going to be God's Love which is eternal and everlasting or the worldly love which is seasonable or just for that moment. It is essential that you know in your spirit which one of these emotional force that's leading you in your walk in life and can you identify which type of spiritual love that dwells in your heart. I know many can relate, when you have a man or woman that will come together with their significant other and engage in some form of intense mind blowing sex that makes them feel out of this world. That sexual energy that traps that feeling and now they think that they are in love. They barely knows anything about that person, their background history, health statues or even their frame of mind but the sex is so great to them that they are actually caught up and blinded by this energy. This phenomenal spiritual force can captivates ones mind and body leaving them in this love lust type of state of mind. But you will also find many that's being caught up in the love of sex, money, power or desperately the need of attention. Many seeking for security that they may be lacking or just desperately seeking loving for whatever reason just to be able to fulfil that inadequacy. This love lust spiritual force is not healthy and definitely not of God. If one doesn't recognize it can destroy their lives or worst take them to their grave. When the devil comes to steal kill and destroy that's what he target is the mind. When he got you believing that love is to hurt someone physical, verbally or mentally you are now caught up in this darkness spiritual realm that only going to bring you misery and destruction in your own life. Unfortunately there are those that don't know how to love or what it is like to be loved. For those that never were taught how to or has not been given that Godly love, including myself, struggles to distinguish between loving a person and being in love with that person. I would like to elaborate more on this later in the chapter. But basically every human needs that since of love and to feel humanize they will take on any force of emotional energy to feel that love. Love does play a powerful role in every human life and the greatest gift that God gave us is his everlasting love. Love is so essential that it is one of God's commands and that is to love our neighbors as we love ourselves. But what happened? At what point in our lives that we let abuse, hatred, lust and other negative energy take control of our hearts and replace this as love. Why do we find it so difficult to walk in love but easy to walk in hate. Turning on the very same one's that sacrifice and give so much of themselves but we tend to hurt them the most. Why do it seems like we wait until we lose that love one before we cry out our love for that person. Then at that point start confessing all the good about that person, wishing and praying that we had one more chance to tell them how much we love them. Here is another spiritual awakening, there is no prayer in this world that will bring them back to us once they pass away. Love suppose to be the love that God intended it to be if we walk in God's perfect love and simply just asking of him. If you wasn't never taught how to love or wasn't shown by example, well the best example to go by would be through the love of our Lord and Savior Jesus Christ.

This emotional force, the spiritual energy makes us who we are. Seeing so many of Gods people stuck confused or just hurting because of the lack of the love of God in their life. Where as many that does have the love of God but still battles with loving or being love by others. In this case we raise the question "Why".

For many reasons this became a task for me, God using me to give some knowledge on this battle of love. Knowing that many are hurting, confused lost or giving/gave up on loving themselves or others. Taking this on I had to face my own battles and pain. My own lack of, receiving, giving and understanding love. Looking back at one point in my life when I was hungry for love but instead it was scattered and destroyed. Those moments during certain times in my life when love ones expressed their love for me, held and caress me, even made passionate love to me and with those very same hands physically abused me. Then there was one that supposed to be the one to give me a better life but instead verbally abused me because of his failure of trying to control my life. Crying out to the Lord again I asked him "Why". Praying and believing, not only those individuals are no

60

longer in my life but because of a better walk with the Lord I am healed. No longer that spirit of anger and pain controls my soul, my broken heart became a forgiving and loving heart. My cry turned into laughter, my soul is now placed with peace and thankfulness. My heart is now open to accept and give the Godly Love that I no longer starving for. I am made whole and one with my Lord and can do all things through Christ who strengthening me. Being ever so grateful for the Holy Spirit and when God answer prayers he will move mountains to make what seem to be impossible...POSSIBLE.

MARK 11:23&24

(23) For verily I say unto you, That whosoever shall say unto this mountain, Be thou removed, and be cast into the sea; and shall not doubt in his heart, but shall believe that those things which he saith shall come to pass; he shall have whatsoever he saith.

(24) Therefore I say unto you, what things so ever ye desire, when you pray, believe that ye receive them, and ye shall have them.

In order for me to hear the voice of God and to be acceptable to his will many love ones, friends and acquaintances had to be removed from my life. Taking on this task God moved stumbling blocks, drama, other people demanding needs of me and negative energy that was clogging up my ears to hear God's voice in my spirit. I was placed in a circle in a environment by myself, left alone but then again in a place with just me and the Holy Spirit. It was like I just woke up one day looked around and everything and everybody was gone. No demands, no comments, drama, negative energy in my space, my life. It was like this positive force of energy took over and I begin to feel free. I knew it was of God because of this great peace that came over me and my life. For the first time my spirit feels alive. The pain that started from childhood that carried into my adulthood, the anger from failed marriages, deceit, lies, abuses, being falsely accused, all just lifted off my spirit and being replaced with a forgiveness heart. At first I didn't understand what was happening. I begin to question God why am I alone. Weeks goes by and now turning into months and nobody comes around, I barely get any calls or response from family and friends. I felt like I was put on a deserted Island with no outside communication. When the Holy Spirit spoke to me to let me know that it is of God's will. Now I begin to understand with great wisdom that poured in my spirit. Him clearing my path allowed me to hear from him and just him at this moment, having a better walk with Jesus in my life and being obedient to the Holy Spirit. Allowing me to speak what is said of God and giving the opportunity through the Holy Spirit of recognize how so many people that's caught up in this worldly love. All the same time hearing the cries, hurt, frustration and pain that people are experiencing over loving someone or just to be loved. Now I understand why so many individuals was coming to me expressing their pain that they are experiencing. God clearing my path to use me to give many a better understanding of this emotional energy force that has people questioning and blinded by it. But being able to share such wisdom and knowledge that the Lord placed in my spirit hopefully can help take away so many people pain and to give many a better understanding. Not an excuse but a better understanding about the meaning of Love.

Let's start off by getting back to what I have mentioned earlier in the chapter. There is this emotional force that give us a character that dwells in our spirit. This love that God intended for us to walk in, his perfect Love is giving to us through the Holy Spirit and by his grace and mercy. Mankind cannot do it by themselves. We were born into a corrupted world that molded us to become imperfect. "For God so loved the world that he gave his only begotten son". He spent down his son, our Lord and Savior who is the truth the way and LIFE. To walk in perfect love is to walk with the Lord and to walk in that love is to fall in love with Jesus. To many of us want to play Church, play with God's word and play games with the devil. He shed his blood, gave his life for us so that we can live and he to live in us. His cry out to the Heavenly Father was to forgive them for they know not what they do. Our perfect and mighty heavenly father forgives us for our sins and his will is to love one another as we love ourselves. To have that Godly love for one another is only through the very same one, our Lord, that loved us first. He gave his life for us and giving our life back to him is the only way to walk in God's perfect Love. We learn by behavior and our environment and many seek to love the world for attention, to gain power or for the love of money. Without the proper guidance of the Holy Spirit people are known to only give back what has been giving to them. Limiting their feeling to love by the way they are being/was loved. I find that so many people expects or want so much from others but are not willing to give half that energy back. If anything they will feed off of other peoples energy for their comfort and to satisfy their needs. If ones need is complete by the Holy Spirit, obeying the will of God and walking with Jesus, there wouldn't be any room in their life to feed off other people's energy. Like a vampire sucking the life from others. God placed me, what I called, This Alone Place by myself at this time and his purpose to allow me to examine my own heart. To strengthen and connecting my spirit as one with the Holy Spirit in order for me to recognize and help many souls that lost, battling and confused with their own spirituality; in God's timing. This journey was the most powerful and rewarding experience that I ever endured in my entire life. As I examine my heart and looking back on my life, I have seen myself grown and matured tremendously. When there were a time when I did not trust anybody but the Lord gave me reasons to believe. When I did not respect others he showed me how to stand on faith through him. When my words was like a weapon that pierced through others hearts and many hearts that was hurt and broken from my actions out of self defense. Even when my heart became cold due to many years of being physically mentally and emotionally abused he shield my heart. When I thought my heart was dead he brought life back into it. When I build that wall and stand to let no one in, his love showered me and through him my strength and trust in him tore down that wall. Now I am free, restored and made whole.

Faithful trustworthy and loyal, first and far most, to my Heavenly Father myself and to others. I am delivered from the hurt and shame of my pass. Transformed and renewed and became as one with the Holy Spirit. Walk with my Lord and Savior and to press everyday to stand in God's perfect will. To give my life to the Lord gave me life again. I now can forgive, walk in joy and to live in such overwhelming peace in my life each and everyday. I am honored and truly humble to share the word of God and to deliver God message to many that are hurting, feeling lost or wants to give up. People please understand it's not about you. You did not create yourself and the things in this world, you ARE NOT going to take anything with you when you leave this world. You can not forgive others if you don't forgive yourself. Again we were born in a corrupted world. We learn by trail and error. Give your pass, your mistakes and your sin to God. To live in the pass is not going to give you a future. Be true to yourself, take off that mask and those blindfolds, only then you can see the path that God wants you to talk and hear his voice to lead you where he wants you to go. The amount of time you spend complaining and stressing, you can use that same energy praying and believing. Stop running to Social Media and putting your life in the hands of others, when all is said and done, those very same ones can't do anything for you. People like to hear themselves talk and may have good intention but truthfully they don't have a heaven or hell to put you in. On the real they barely have a pot for them to piss in. It is God's will to forgive and to love one another. Help, edify and build each other up. But it has to start from you. What measure you meet will be giving back to you. Don't be so caught up believing that as long as you giving people "Your Money" you are doing enough and giving "Your Money" will win you points to get you into Heaven. Have you thought about giving of your time, sometimes just to listen to that love one. Your heart to simply say I love and appreciate you and to be just as loyal and respectful as you want to be giving unto you.

LUKE 6:38

Give, and it shall be given unto you; good measure, pressed down, and shaken together and running over, shall men give into your bosom. For with the same measure that ye mete withal it shall be measured to you again.

Take that trip on that deserted Island. Leave everything and everyone behind. Search your heart, be real and true to yourself. Give yourself that 100%. Don't give up...give in.

Surrender your life to the same one that gave you life. Listen to the voice of God and his calling and purpose for your life. Then will your eyes be open to see any deceitful spirits that try's to keep you down and sucking the life out of you. Know the difference between Holy Spirit and the spirit of the devil. Now when you feel completed and one with God, you can step into "The ways of the World" knowing that you don't have to be a footstool to be walked all over. Excepting yourself as being label a "Bitch" or being someone's "Nigga". Falling as a victim to that deceitful false loved to be mistreated abused and then tossed away. Some people means well but again they can't give you 100% when they barely giving themselves 50% and under the same breath if you want 100% then you need to give 100%. To the rich and famous or the individuals that's getting that paper (NICE MONEY) legally or illegally, money may buy you happiness but it can't buy you that ticket to heaven. Rich poor white black believer or a nonbeliever of God...etc., if you want respect you have to give respect. If you want to be loved you need to show love. Look at that person carefully in the mirror. You cannot do right by anyone if you don't do right by the one that's looking back at you in that mirror. To give that 100% to yourself or anybody else, YOU have to start by giving it all to him. He is that very same one that gave you life in the first place. When you open up your heart and give your life to Jesus your spirit becomes connects and made one with the Lord. He is our protector, provider, healer, our Alpha and Omega the beginning and our end. People dry those tears, pray on being delivered from that angry spirit, stop the complaining and creating drama. Start walking in love and not hate against one another. Learn to control your finances and not money controlling you. Gain that power over your own soul. Meet yourself on that deserted Island and what you will find is that Island is not so deserted after all. The real "YOU" will be there waiting and everything you need and want will be there waiting to greet you.

# Chapter 11

# THE LAST DAYS

If one have not been made aware yet the time is near. The warning signs are here as we are facing the last days. As it was mention in the bible, in the beginning Jesus sat with God when he spoke; "Let's make man in OUR image". It was done. As the time is near Jesus will return for his people, God's will…will be done. He is the Alpha and Omega the beginning and the end.

But yet many walks with blind folds across their eyes and ear plugs in their ears. They hear and see but they chose not to believe. So many unbelievers are caught up in their own world, enjoying their world of lust and worldly pleasure seeking for materials and worldly riches. Falling into a world of Idolatry, pulling more away from the love of God but drawing in by the lies of the devil. As where you have those who think that they are saved by just "believing" in Jesus. As a result they continue to live worldly sinful lives with no real conversation taking place in their heart.

## 2 TIMOTHY 3:1-4

(1) This know also, that in the last days perilous times shall come

(2) For men shall be lovers of their own selves, covetous, boasters, proud, blasphemers, disobedient to parents, unthankful, unholy.

(3) Without natural affection, trucebreakers, false accusers of those that are good.

(4) Traitors, heady, high-minded, lovers of pleasures more than lovers of God.

This I say, exam your own heart and take a good look at that person in the mirror. The next time you have that urge to question how's the next person is living, check out what's going on in your household first. How many believers (children of God) actually are studying God's Word or praying but yet spends countless time watching TV, on the computer, playing video games (and those are just the adults) on the phone and/ or texting (caught up in drama) and most of all that countless time that is spent on Social Media. As people continues to get caught up more and more with themselves or the drama of other people lives they are blinded to what is right in front of them. They are actually losing themselves and the control over their own household. It looks like the kids are taking over, which suppose to be our future but hypothetically can't even tie their own shoes. I guess looking back in my days as a child it was that strong walk of obedience, respect and discipline in the household and to our elders. I can't believe that there are so many of our young children that don't even know what that means. I surely know that the time is near and beginning of the end is here when you have so many walks of life with NO COMMON SENSE. From adult to the young children.

You would think that common sense will tell a person, If you are texting and driving the chances are... If you are a parent or guardian and you leave the child in the car alone the chances are... If you use the bathroom especially after a bowel movement and don't wash your hands the chances are... I can go on and on but I am sure that the point was made. I do want to bring one more thing to the light. Women young and older if you meet a man in a club, a social lounge or even through social media please...please understand if he is offering you drinks and to go back to his house all means of the morning hours, he is not taking you there for conversation. So many walked away cried rape but unfortunately some never walked away at all and is not here today to tell their side of the story. People wants to blame the devil for everything that is negative. Stop giving the devil so much power. Certain things are just simply common sense but unfortunately as simply as it may seems some people just don't have it. People we need a Spiritual Awakening. We are living in the days of Revelation. Not only there are the lost of souls but look around at the devastation and destruction that we are facing around the world today. From the devastating of earthquakes, tornadoes, tsunami to the change of our global warming. Old and new diseases that claimed and will claim the lives of many people to mankind believing what's evil is good and what's good is evil. So after what's going on around the world today and the end is near do you think humans and species of all kind should still continue to be fruitful and multiple?. Through the hatred and deceiving from mankind one to another, animals that bringing forth new breed of life from other animals that's not of its own kind. Hunger and salvation that claiming the lives of children that dying before they even begin to live. From Wars that started from beginning of time to new War that will claim the lives of numerous of people as predicted. Raising of eyebrows and questioning why bring forth children and animals into this world in this day and time only to suffer and die. Many questions but NOT enough answers. Apart from all this devastation and tragedy that going on around the world and within ones own self, it will be that moment when it all ends. In a moment, in a twinkling of an eye, with the second coming of our Lord Jesus Christ. Where there'll be no more suffering and pain, no sickness nor sin but that instantaneous transformation of our bodies to fit us for eternity. NO OTHER THAN THE RAPTURE.

### 1 THESSALONIANS 4:16-17

(16) For the Lord himself will descend from heaven with a shout, with the voice of the archangel, and with God's trumpet. The dead in Christ will rise first.

(17) then we who are alive, who are left, will be caught up together with them in the clouds, to meet the Lord in the air. So we will be with the Lord forever.

The rapture of the church is a glorious event we should all be longing for. We will finally be free from sin. HOWEVER IF ONE BELIEVE OR DON'T BELIEVE GOD'S WILL...WILL BE DONE.

People we have to wake up, more so then ever. Not only that we are in the last days, but no man knows the day or hour when Jesus returns. He will appear like a theft in the night, coming for his Church. So if you are not ready then guess what...YOU DON'T WANT TO BE LEFT BEHIND.

As part of my profession in the medical field I have dealt with so many people unfortunately when on their death bed spoke about their lives and the life style that they were living. Those that had just about everything they wanted and needed (but did not have Jesus in their lives) spoke about all the goods and riches that they had but mention of how they felt this means of inadequate and loneliness. They conversation was as if they was missing something or never felt completed. Listening to them was like hearing their souls crying out for help. As where those that accepted the Lord in their lives, had a personal relationship with him and to the best of their ability walked with the Lord, felt rested and at peace. They did not have much money, material things or even closeness of family and friends but they spoke about feeling completed and full. I can even recall having a conversation with one of my sisters and as we dialogue, we came to an understanding through life experiences knowing some friends of ours that was fortunate enough to have been or is financially comfortable. But appears to be the ones that's most unhappy and uncomfortable in their walk without the Lord. I have also found that during the 17 years of experience in the hospitals and nursing homes I have seen the drastic changes in patients over time, especially in the nursing homes. It went from more than half of the percentage being elders as residents or patients to now being a much younger population of men and women residing in nursing homes facility. It's not because of old age anymore. You have the middle age and even a lot more young age adults resisting there due to life threatening or chronic illness that family/friends can't assist them at home. Again people we are in the last days and all signs of the second coming of Jesus is here. What was is no longer and what's to come is here. It will get worst before it gets better. Jesus is the only way. To be either Spiritual Awaken or Spiritual dead, which path are you walking through.

I have lived long enough to see so many people suffering day by day. Lost confused and even giving up on life. At one point having a friend that actually wanted to give up and try to comment suicide. One of the worst experience ever. When having a conversation on the phone with him and he's telling me that he had a gun to his head. I was able to talk him down through the help of the Holy Spirit. We did speak a few more times within a couple of weeks but shortly after that we lost contact. With no results at all trying to contact with him I had to pray and give it over to the Lord. Knowing that suicide is not the will of God but of sin and the way of destruction, death and damnation. As much as we have many that are mentally strong there are just as much that are mentally weak. Your spirit is who you are and when the spirit dies the body follows. Remember the time is here and the last days are near. Give back to God what God gave unto you...LIFE. Become one with the spirit of The Heavenly Father, our Lord and Savior Jesus Christ and The Holy Spirit.

# THE MESSAGE

In the Beginning God created...

He is The Alpha and Omega the beginning and the end. All things were made through him. Without him was not anything made that has been made (John 1:3).

I give my Heavenly Father thanks and forever grateful for this book. He is the Author and Creator of Spiritual Awakening through the Holy Spirit.

I present this book as a message and its purpose to help wake up many souls. Souls that live but yet walks around asleep. As many has chosen not to believe in the Word of God, there are others who try to play God and/or play with God's word. Hearts that still stand harden with unforgiveness and hearts that's walks around with such anger and selfishness. Unbelievers that's serving the god of this world and choosing to do the work of the devil. Wake up God's children; this is not the day and time to be asleep. It's time to take off those blind folds and ear plugs out of your ears. Look around and be vigilant we are fighting this spiritual warfare that's killing the spirit, the holy spirit within you, day by day. As we are born to live we are born to die. Unfortunately many are spiritually dead as their body dies without a fighting chance. Never got the chance to live out God's full potential and/or purpose for their lives. Be knowledgeable of God's plan and purpose for you. He created us we did not created him. As of those who got it twisted that trying to play god, serving two masters, talking out both sides of their mouths, playing this love and hate game or even going as far as hurting or taking innocent lives. God stands in the midst of every action that projects out of all mankind. Nothing that is made, all that is made cannot stands without the Power of God. Rise and awaken sleeping spirits. Children of God without the Holy Spirit the flesh cannot stand alone. Through the power of God stand as prayer warriors and put on the faith of God. United together under the Spirit of God to take on this darkness and deceiving spirits that got people twisted, thinking that all things was created for them. Let's get a better understanding, God created us for a purpose, his purpose and to be under his will. Now some choose to work for a Master/Boss, some chose to work for themselves and other may chose to not work at all. It becomes a blessing when it is lined up in the will of God. Seek ye first the Kingdom of God, and his righteousness and all these things shall be added unto you (Matthew 6:33). It's good to serve your boss, it's good to serve yourself and it's a great thing to help others but PUT GOD FIRST. Know what his purpose and calling is for you and your life. Shut down the flesh and rise up the spirit. Have a personal relationship with him and give no room for the devil. Stop giving him so much credit and power over your lives. Give it all to God; repent, confess and believe. Stop settling for what life throws at you. Stop trying to do it your way and by yourself. Have you not learn yet that your way is not the way. All the babies that you have created, all the titles that you hold, all the degrees that you walked away with and even down to your riches and fame does not make you the creator. These things will pass but the love of God is everlasting. Put away the suffering, the hurt and pain, the lies and deceit. Get rid of the anger and hatred and put on a forgiven heart. The first step to an awaken and a peaceful spirit is to accept Jesus Christ as your Lord and Savior. I am the way, the truth and life; no man cometh unto the Father, but by me (John 14:6). He was wounded for our transgressions, he was bruised for our iniquities; the chastisement of our peace was upon him; and with his stripes we are healed. (Isaiah 53: 5). Many has lost their way and became side track, like the Twilight Zone, end up right back where they started from. To walk in a righteous path take up your cross, know that Jesus is the way and the only way. Let's take this down a notch, a little out of the spiritual realm and more into the natural, to give a better understanding to those who are slow at taking off their blind folds. God love us so that he breathe into our lungs to give us life. He gave us his only begotten son to be under one spirit with the FATHER, SON AND THE HOLY SPIRIT. God's will is for us to do his will and what's pleasing unto him, knowing that your name is in the book of life. Give him the greatest love that he gave you...your Life. The world cannot be save but your soul can. Wake up sleeping spirit, take off your blind folds, put down your weapons and put on the Armour of God. Fight in prayer, walk in the faith, seek your purpose and God's will for you. Love one another as you love yourself. Since we tried it every other way now lets try it God's way.

Made in the USA
Middletown, DE
25 March 2018